BBC earth

DO YOU KNOW?

Level 4

FAST AND SLOW

Inspired by BBC Earth TV series and developed with input from BBC Earth natural history specialists

Written by Camilla de la Bedoyere
Text adapted by Hannah Fish
Series Editor: Nick Coates

LADYBIRD BOOKS

UK | USA | Canada | Ireland | Australia
India | New Zealand | South Africa

Ladybird Books is part of the Penguin Random House group of companies
whose addresses can be found at global.penguinrandomhouse.com.
www.penguin.co.uk   www.puffin.co.uk   www.ladybird.co.uk

Penguin
Random House
UK

First published 2020
001

Printed in China

A CIP catalogue record for this book is available from the British Library

ISBN: 978-0-241-35579-4

All correspondence to:
Ladybird Books Ltd
Penguin Random House Children's
One Embassy Gardens, New Union Square
5 Nine Elms Lane, London SW8 5DA

Contents

New words

dive
(verb)

hunt
(verb)

insect

mammal

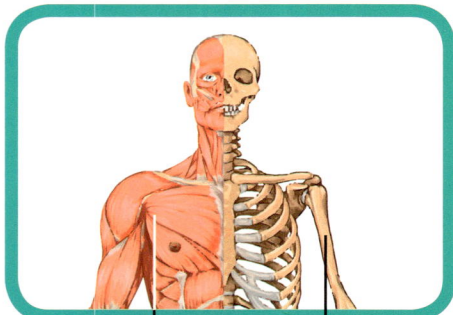

muscle   **bone**

predator

prey
(noun)

seabed

skeleton

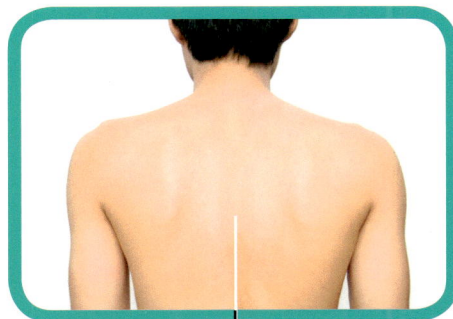

skin

speed

spine

How do animals move?

An animal uses **muscles** to move its body. When muscles get shorter, they pull on part of the body and make it move.

Vertebrates are animals with **bones**. Muscles pull on the bones to make them move.

Bats, dolphins and cheetahs are vertebrates. They each have a **skeleton** and muscles.

Invertebrates are animals with no bones. Many invertebrates have hard **skin**. Muscles pull on the hard skin.

This crab is an invertebrate. Its hard shell is like a skeleton.

Work in a group. Make a table of vertebrates and invertebrates. Think of three examples of each type of animal. How do they move?

7

Which animals need speed?

Some animals move fast when they want to catch food. Animals can also move fast when a **predator** is running after them!

Wolves and bison can run for a long time before they get tired.

Wolves are predators.

Wolves have long legs and thin bodies, which are good for running fast.

Wolves **hunt** in groups.

Some wolves hunt bison.
They can run after the
bison for up to 32 kilometres.
The bison get tired and the
wolves can catch them.

Bison eat plants.
They are large animals
with strong muscles.

▶ WATCH!

Watch the video (see page 32).
Why do the wolves try to catch a baby bison?
How does the mother bison protect her baby?

9

How slow is a sloth?

A sloth is very slow! This three-toed sloth is the slowest **mammal** in the world. It takes a long time to walk a metre!

Sloths move so slowly that little plants grow in their fur. The plants make the sloths look green.

fur

Sloths walk and climb slowly, but they are very good swimmers.

Sloths and koalas do not need **speed**. They eat plants, and plants cannot run away!

Koalas sleep for most of the day.

Koalas live in trees and eat leaves.

LOOK!

Look at the pages.
Why do sloths look green?

Why don't tortoises need speed?

Many slow animals do not need speed. They have other ways to stay safe.

Tortoises do not need speed. They eat plants, and they have a hard shell that stops predators eating them.

Toads do not need to move fast. A toad's skin is bad to eat, so most predators do not hunt them.

A bumblebee flies slowly. But the yellow on the bee's body tells birds that the bee can hurt them, so birds do not catch the bee.

Sea urchins move slowly, too. They have **spines** that stop most predators eating them.

THINK!

Elephants and rhinos are large animals that usually walk slowly. How do they stay safe without running away?

What flies fast?

There are three groups of animals that fly: birds, bats and **insects**.

Flying animals use their wings to fly. They need strong muscles.

Birds with long, large wings fly high in the sky. When a golden eagle **dives**, it is one of the fastest birds in the world.

Hummingbirds are small birds. They move their wings faster than any other bird.

The fastest bird in the world is the peregrine falcon.

▶ **WATCH!**

Watch the video (see page 32).
How fast can a golden eagle fly when it dives?

Are all cats quick movers?

All cats can move fast. They are predators, and they use speed to catch their **prey**.

The fastest cat is the cheetah. It has a top speed of 96 kilometres an hour. It can only run for a short time before it gets tired!

A cheetah's body is perfect for speed. It has long, thin legs. It can change direction quickly.

Leopards walk slowly and quietly.

Then, suddenly, they jump on their prey!

▶ **WATCH!**

Watch the video (see page 32).
How fast can a tiger run?

Which animals are the fastest swimmers?

These fish swim fast. Their bodies are perfect for moving through water.

A fast fish is long and thin. It has a strong tail with lots of muscles. A fish uses its tail to push through the water. Its tail moves from side to side.

The yellowfin tuna has a top speed of 60 kilometres an hour.

Sea lions are not fish, but their bodies are long and strong. They are fast swimmers, too.

Sea lions hunt yellowfin tuna. The sea lions can change direction fast.

FIND OUT!

Sea lions are not fish. **Use books or the internet** to find out what kind of animals they are.

These animals also live in water.

Sea stars move slowly along the **seabed** using their five arms. They look for something to eat.

Turtles are good swimmers. They swim a long way to the beaches where they lay their eggs.

Jellyfish are not good swimmers. As the water moves, it takes the jellyfish with it.

Seahorses are very slow fish. They use their tails to hold on to plants. Then, the water cannot take them with it!

🔍 LOOK!

Look at the pages.
How many arms does a sea star have?
Are jellyfish good swimmers?

21

Why do penguins walk slowly?

Penguins walk slowly because their legs are short.

A penguin is a bird, but it does not fly. Its wings are too small. A penguin uses its wings to swim fast to catch fish.

The fastest swimming bird is the gentoo penguin.

When a penguin is out of the water, it does not need speed. Penguins live in very cold places where there are not many predators.

Penguins can slide on ice and snow. It is faster than walking, and more fun!

PROJECT

Work in a group.
Explore ways that toy cars can roll easily over a smooth surface, like a tray. If you cover the tray with sand or water, do the cars move faster or slower?

Which lizard has a fast tongue?

Chameleons are lizards.
They have very fast tongues.

Most chameleons live in trees.
They move slowly so predators do not see them.

When a chameleon sees an insect, it slowly moves near.

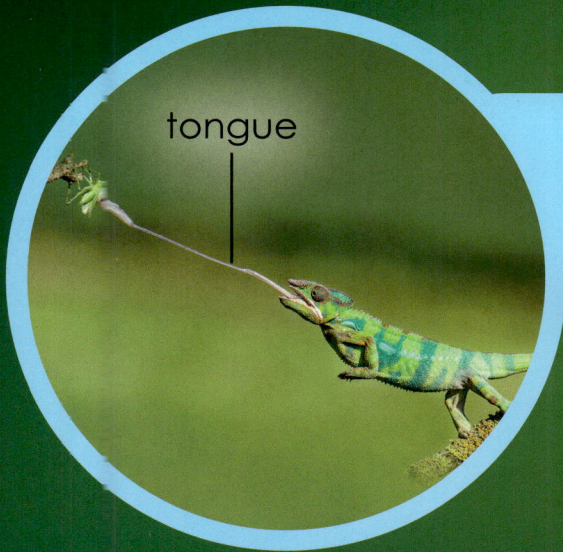

tongue

Suddenly, the chameleon's long tongue comes out of its mouth. It catches the insect with its tongue!

Other animals move suddenly, too.

This praying mantis is an insect. It waits until its prey is near. Then, its front legs quickly move and catch its prey.

A praying mantis can wait a long time for an insect to catch.

THINK!

Why do you think the praying mantis has spines on its front legs?

25

Which shark is the fastest?

All sharks are predators, but they have different ways of catching food.

Some sharks hide and swim slowly near the seabed. Then, they suddenly move fast to catch their prey.

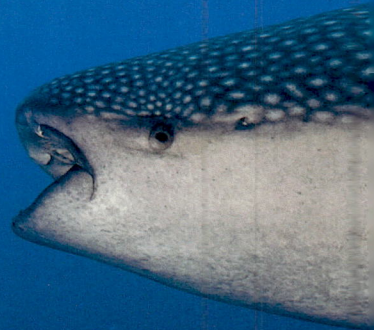

wobbegong

The wobbegong can hide on the seabed.

Sharks can be very fast swimmers. The shortfin mako has a top speed of over 80 kilometres an hour. It hunts fast prey, like dolphins and tuna.

The whale shark is the world's largest fish. It does not swim fast because it eats very small animals.

THINK!

One of the sharks on this page is the fastest shark in the world. Which one is the fastest? How fast can it swim?

What slithers and what swings?

Snakes slither along the ground because they do not have legs or wings. But they do have lots of strong muscles. Snakes can move very fast if they need to.

The black mamba can slither faster than you can run! It has a top speed of 19 kilometres an hour.

Worms, snails and slugs can also slither, but they cannot move fast.

Gibbons are apes that swing through trees.

Gibbons have big muscles in their arms. They need strong arms to swing fast.

PROJECT

Work in a group.
Find four fast animals in this book. Put them in a list in order of speed. Use books or the internet to research some of the other animals in the book. Find their top speeds and add them to your list.

Quiz

Choose the correct answers.

1 An animal with no bones is called . . .
   a a vertebrate.
   b an invertebrate.
   c a muscle.

2 Some wolves eat . . .
   a bison.
   b wolves.
   c plants.

3 Which of these sentences is NOT true?
   a Sloths and koalas eat plants.
   b Sloths can swim well.
   c Koalas are the slowest mammals
      in the world.

4 Which of these sentences is NOT true?
   a Cheetahs use their speed to catch prey.
   b Cheetahs can run fast for a short time.
   c Cheetahs can run fast for a long time.

5 Which animals are the best swimmers?
   a sea stars
   b seahorses
   c turtles

6 A penguin is fastest when . . .
   a swimming.
   b walking.
   c flying.

7 Which of these sentences is NOT true?
   a A chameleon is a kind of lizard.
   b Chameleons move fast in trees.
   c A chameleon catches insects
      with its tongue.

8 Snakes can move fast because . . .
   a they slither along the ground.
   b they do not have legs or wings.
   c they have lots of strong muscles.

Visit www.ladybirdeducation.co.uk for
FREE **DO YOU KNOW?** teaching resources.

- video clips with simplified voiceover and subtitles
- video and comprehension activities
- class projects and lesson plans
- audio recording of every book
- digital version of every book
- full answer keys

To access video clips, audio tracks and digital books:

1 Go to **www.ladybirdeducation.co.uk**
2 Click "Unlock book"
3 Enter the code below

K5Mx7oTIj9

Stay safe online! Some of the DO YOU KNOW? activities ask children to do extra research online. Remember:

- ensure an adult is supervising;
- use established search engines such as Google or Kiddle;
- children should never share personal details, such as name, home or school address, telephone number or photos.